Christmas Tree Crochet For Adults

Many Beautiful Christmas Tree Patterns For Beginners

Copyright © 2020

DEDICATION

Contents

Crochet Christmas Tree Ornament

The Crochet Christmas Tree Ornament is such a fun project and a great way to add some holiday cheer to your home. This is a quick pattern to whip up in everyone's favorite corner-to-corner technique and it uses minimal amounts of yarn. These would make great gifts, a bunting, or hanging on your tree too. I hope you will give this a try. Scroll down for the free crochet pattern.

The yarn is by Yarnspirations, called Red Heart Soft in the color Guacamole, Red Heart Chic Sheep by Marly Bird in the color Leather, and Caron Simply Soft in the color White.

Stitches used are (C2C) double crochet corner-to-corner, and the Thermal single crochet stitch with video tutorials on both of them. This easy pattern is really fun to make and to decorate.

The original tree I made didn't have a back to it which didn't look very nice. I decided to make two trees and sew them together. Plus weaving in all those ends took forever! This solved both of my problems: only two ends to weave in, and it looks great from all sides.

Make two clusters in each size, 8 panels in total. These whip up really fast!

I didn't add any stuffing inside but you could add some to make it bigger if you like. All the ends are placed inside the tree to make it appear stuffed. Weaving in the ends is not my favorite part so this makes me happy that we could skip that part.

Skill Level: Easy, with knowledge of C2C technique.

Supplies:

Yarn: Red Heart Soft – Color A: Quacamole 45 yards

Yarn: Caron Simply Soft – Color B: White 25 yards

Yarn: Chic Sheep by Marly Bird – Color C: Leather 5 yards

Crochet Hook: 5.00 mm (H/8)

Yarn Needle

Yarn Information:

Yarn weight: #4, Worsted Weight

Fiber: Acrylic

Chic Sheep Yarn: Fiber – Wool.

Abbreviations: In US Terminology

beg – beginning

ch – chain

dc – double crochet

sc – single crochet

sl st – slip stitch

sp(s) – space(s)

st(s) – stitch(es)

WS – wrong side

Special Stitches:

Cluster – Ch 3 and 3 dc in same space (1 cluster). See C2C

Thermal single crochet (tsc): Insert hook in blo of next st and insert hook in the open loop from one row below, yo, pull through, yo, pull through both loops on hook. (1 tsc). See tsc

Gauge: 4 rows x 2.5 clusters = 3 inches.

Measurement: 7" high by 6.5" wide, excludes hanging loop.

Notes:

1. Worked in Rows, turn after each row.

2. Stitch counts are in ( ) brackets at the ends of the Rows.

INSTRUCTIONS:

Please read through the entire pattern before starting.

C2C PANELS: (8 Total)

Make 2 Panels in each size. Cluster count at the bottom row: 2 Clusters, 3 Clusters, 4 Clusters, 5 Clusters.

Color A – Chain 6, turn.

Row 1: 1 dc in 4th ch from hook, 1 dc in next 2 chs. (1 cluster).

Row 2: Ch 6, 1 dc in 4th ch from hook, 1 dc in next 2 chs, turn, sl st in next ch 3 sp, ch 3, 3 dc in same ch-3 space. (2 clusters).

End off yarn-leave tail for seaming, set aside. Make 2 panels.

3 Clusters: Repeat above instructions through Row 2. Repeat Row 2 one more time. (3 clusters). End off yarn-leave tail for seaming, set aside. Make 2 panels.

4 Clusters: Repeat above instructions through Row 2. Repeat Row 2 two more times. (4 clusters). End off yarn-leave tail for seaming, set aside. Make 2 panels.

5 Clusters: Repeat above instructions through Row 2. Repeat Row 2 three more times. (5 clusters). End off yarn-leave tail for seaming, set aside. Make 2 panels.

EDGING:

Color B

With a slip knot on your hook, sl st to top of panel. *Ch 1, sl st in next st*, repeat *-* around entire panel. End with a sl st in beg st. End off yarn.

Repeat for all 8 panels.

TRUNK:

Color C – Chain 7

Row 1: sc in 2nd ch from hook, 1 sc in each st across. (6 sc).

Rows 2 – 11: Ch 1, turn, 1 tsc in each st across. (6 tsc).

Row 12: Ch 1, turn, 1 tsc through both loops plus open loop one row below, in each st across. (6 tsc).

End off yarn, weave in bottom end.

SEAMING

Color A – Using tail from one panel.

Tack each tree together separately (see below). Start with one, 5 and 4-cluster panel, sew them together along the edge in Color A. Next, add 3-cluster panel on top of 4-cluster panel and tack it on, then add 2-cluster panel on top of the 3-cluster panel and tack it on. Repeat for other tree.

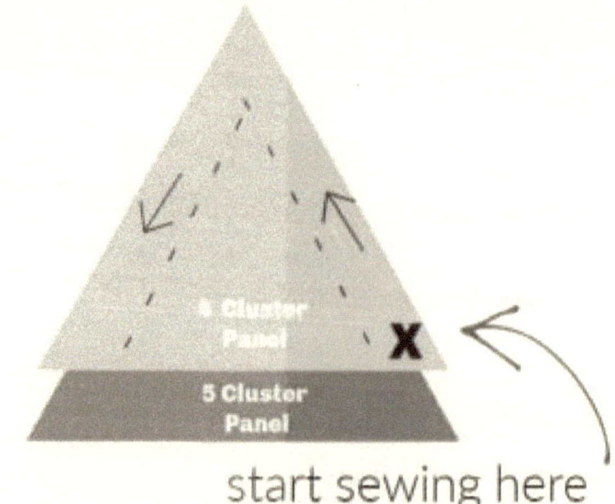

Repeat for 3-cluster panel, and 2-cluster panel.

Color B – cut approximately 2 yards, thread it on your yarn needle.

Place all the loose ends on the wrong side of the trees. Face the WS of both trees together, like a sandwich. With Color B, start at the top of the tree, sew the two trees together along one side, sewing just below the white stitches. Place the trunk where you want it. Sew the bottom of tree and trunk together, and continue to sew up the other side, ending at the top of the tree. Remove the yarn needle. With crochet hook, pick up a loop of the yarn at the top of the tree. Chain 11, pull yarn through last chain to end off. With yarn needle, make the loop at the top. End off yarn, weave in end.

Embellish:

To embellish this little tree, you can add beads to it, or make a garland to go around it. Or how about add some stuffing inside to make it even fatter? I can't wait to see how you decorate your Christmas tree!

Crochet Ribbon Christmas Tree Pattern

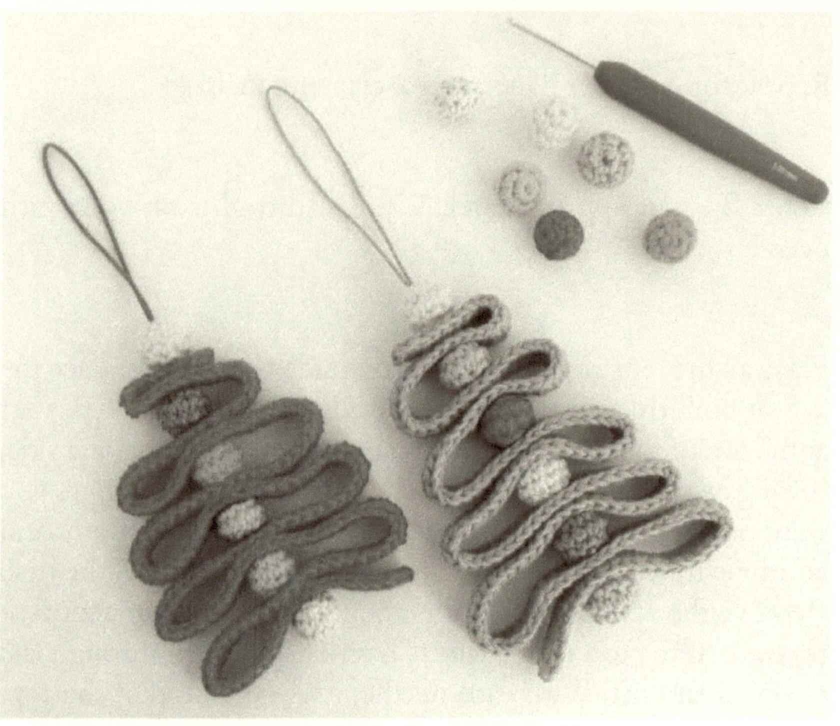

Hello friends ☺

Can you believe it's nearly Christmas !? Nope. Me either! My head is still firmly stuck way back in June somewhere and I'm not at all ready to start thinking about Turduckens or Christmas cheer.

Despite my un-christmasy mood, I've put together a quick and easy pattern for you to deck your halls (or tree).

So without further ado here 'tis…

Crochet Ribbon Christmas Tree

Finished size: 13 cm

What you'll need:

3 mm hook

Small amounts 8 ply/DK cotton yarn. I've used various brands from my stash but a stiffer cotton works better than a soft cotton for these.

Aprox 13g for the tree

Aprox 3 g each in 6 different colours for the baubles

Yarn needle

Tip: You can use any weight yarn for these but they will turn out a different size. Use a hook smaller than you normally would for your yarn so that your work is nice and firm.

US Terms Used (UK/Aus terms in brackets)

Abbreviations:

ch –   chain

sc (dc) –   single crochet (double crochet)

hdc (htr) – half double crochet (half treble)

ss –   slip stitch

Pattern

Tree – Make 1

Foundation row: Ch 182

Row 1: Hdc (htr) into 3rd ch from hook, hdc (htr) up to last ch, 5 hdc (htr) into last ch

Row 2: Turn work upside down and work into bottom loop of ch, hdc (htr) up to last st, 4 hdc (htr) into last st. Join with a ss into top of beginning ch-2. Fasten off and weave ends in.

Baubles – make 6

Worked in spiral rounds

Start: Leaving a long tail (about an arms length) to be used for stuffing later, make a magic circle

Round 1: working into ring, ch 1 (not counted as a st), 6 sc (dc)

Round 2: 2 sc (dc) into each st (12 sc/dc)

Round 3: 12 sc (dc)

Round 4: * skip one st, sc (dc) into next st. Repeat from * 5 more times, stopping half way to insert stuffing (roll long yarn tail into a rough ball shape and squish into half closed ball. Use the blunt end of your hook to help push it all in before you finish closing). Join with a ss.

Fasten off and bury yarn end back up through centre of ball. Clip closely.

Assembly:

Step 1: Lay your tree piece out on a flat surface and fold end back aprox 8.5 cm

Step 2: Keep folding up, making each fold slightly shorter than the last until it looks something like this

Step 3: Place your first bauble at the base of your tree and continue up, placing baubles between 2 layers of each fold (see pic). You'll probably have to fiddle a bit to get your folds looking right (and will need to fiddle even more when you start sewing in a minute)

When you're happy with your tree shape, thread your needle with a length of yarn aprox 40 cm, using the colour of your choice (this will also become the hanging loop)

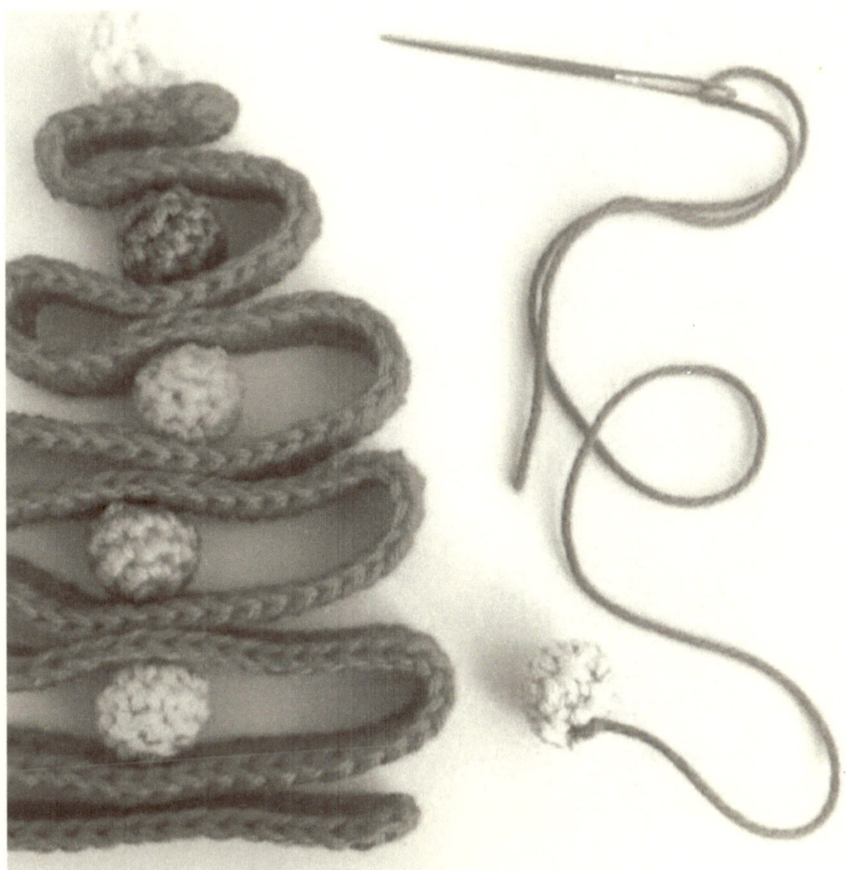

Step 4: Starting with the bottom bauble, secure your thread with a couple of small stitches in the centre top of the bauble (you won't see this as this side will rest up against the bottom of the tree)

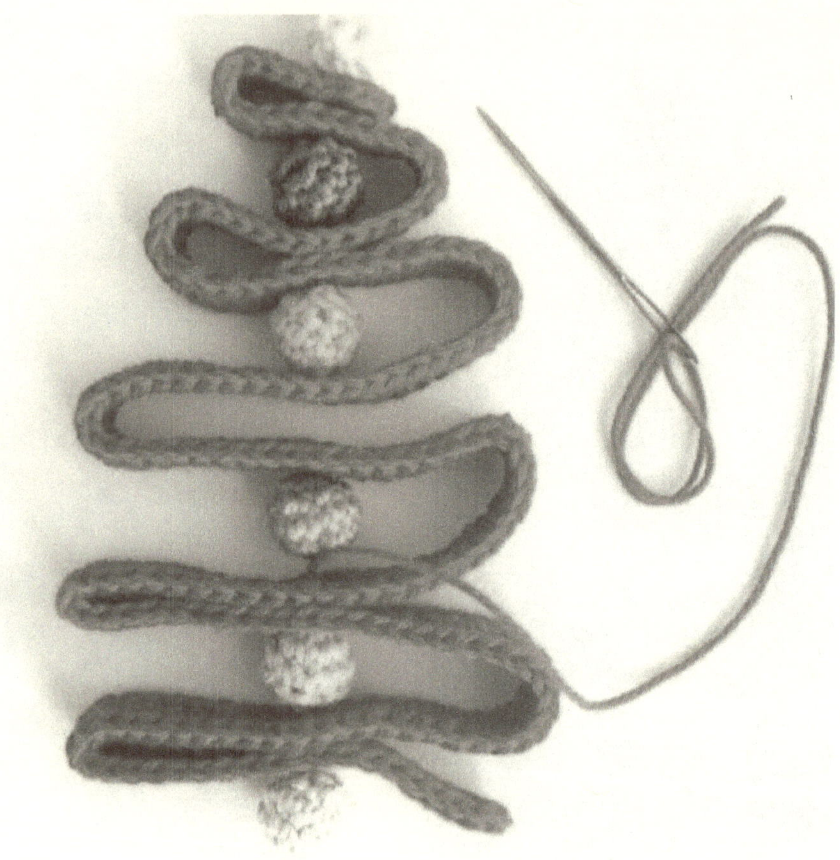

Step 5: Take your needle up through the first layers, pick up your next bauble and run needle up through the centre and then through the next set of layers.

Continue joining together this way until all baubles are

Step 6: Give the tail end a little tug to tighten (don't pull too hard or you'll squish your baubles out of shape).

Step 7: Make a hanging loop with the remaining yarn by going back down through the centre of the top bauble and make a few small stitches into the bottom of the bauble and the top layer of the tree to secure.

Give your tree a little 'foof' and hang for everyone to admire.

Crochet Christmas Tree Pattern

Part 1- CONE

You will need;

K or L hook for 2 strand trees (my white one) I used an L hook.

5 oz of each color should do it, but have more on hand just in case.

Any size hook for single strand.

I used an I hook.

You need about half a skein for a tree. My skeins are 7 oz.

While making the cone, join all rounds with a slip stitch in top of beg ch3.

*** For each round, follow from * to * to finish each round.***

CONE

1. Using a magic ring make the circle, ch 3, 5 dc in ring. Join with sl st in top of ch3. Pull to tighten ring. (6dc)

2. ch3, dc in same st, *1dc in next st, 2 dc in next st* , around.

3. ch3, dc in same st, dc in each of next 2 sts, *2dc in next st, dc in each of next 2 sts* around.

4. ch3, dc in same st, dc in next 3 sts, * 2dc in next st, dc in next 3 sts*, around.

5. dc in each st around.

6. ch3, dc in same st, dc in next 4 sts, * 2dc in next st, dc in next 4 sts* around.

7. ch3, dc in same st, dc in next 5 sts, * 2dc in next st, dc in next 5 sts* around.

8. ch3, dc in same st, dc in next 6 sts, * 2dc in next st, dc in next 6 sts* around.

9. ch3, dc in same st, dc in next 7 sts, * 2dc in next st, dc in next 7 sts* around.

10. ch3, dc in same st, dc in next 8 sts, * 2dc in next st, dc in next 8 sts* around.

11. dc in each st around.

12. ch3, dc in same st, dc in next 9 sts, * 2dc in next st, dc in next 9 sts* around.

13. ch3, dc in same st, dc in next 10 sts, * 2dc in next st, dc in next 10 sts* around.

14. ch3, dc in same st, dc in next 11 sts, * 2dc in next st, dc in next 11 sts* around.

15. ch3, dc in same st, dc in next 12 sts, * 2dc in next st, dc in next 12 sts* around.

16. dc in each st around.

DO NOT FINISH OFF, you will keep going with the branches now.

Part 2- Branches

Branches

While still joined where you slip stitched last row of the cone part, you are going to slip stitch into the post(dc) from the last round (turning your cone sideways) and then slip stitch again into the post(dc) from the previous round. You actually totally skip the whole last row. You will be making the branches between the rows where my needles is in the pic below.

OK now, this is probably the hardest part, trying to explain where to put these branches! But once you get the hang of the pattern, you can go with easily, and should be able to make the next tree with no pattern! :)

Holding your cone upside down (wide part up)

1st branch! You will be doing treble(tr) stitches for a few rows, so wrap yarn around hook 2 times, then push your needle where mine is in the picture above, between the last 2 rows on the cone. Continue your tr st, ch1, tr, ch1, tr, ch1, tr, ch3, tr, ch1, tr, ch1, tr, ch1, tr, ch1. Now, looking back into where you just made this branch, count over 4 posts(dc) and sc into the same area between the rows (as in picture 1). Ch1. Counting over 4 more posts, your going to make another branch. Each branch will be this;

tr, ch1

tr, ch1

tr, ch1

tr, ch3

tr, ch1

tr, ch1

tr, ch1

tr, ch1

And your branch will look like the one in Picture 2 below.

Counting over 4 posts, sc, ch1. count over 4 more posts, make another branch. Keep going around like this until you are back to the first branch, then you simply step up a level, since you are working in a spiral to the top (from the bottom up!)

First Couple Rows

After spiraling around for 4 rows of branches, your tree should look like this one.

Or, if you have a silly little boy like mine, you have just made a most interesting hat for him!

Hmmm, this last pic didn't come out very good.

Now after 4 rows of treble branches, you're ready to do dc branches.

So now each branch will get a little smaller, and the rows will go quicker too!

Each branch now will go like this;

dc, ch1,

dc, ch1,

dc, ch1,

dc, ch2 (ch3 for more pointy branches if you like)

dc, ch1

dc, ch1

dc, ch1

And you will now only skip 3 posts between branches. Try to make sure your branches are not lining up over each row, you don't want them in perfect rows over each other. You can adjust how many posts you skip between branches to get the next branch where you want it. This pattern is very flexible in this way.

You want 3 spiraled rows of dc branches.

Getting near the middle!

Hopefully your tree is looking somewhat like this silly boy's hat!So you now have 4 rows treble branches

3 rows dc branches.

Ok, now we're going to make those branches even smaller!

Each branch will now go like this;

dc, ch1

dc, ch1

dc, ch2

dc, ch1

dc, ch1

dc, ch1

And you can skip 2-3 posts between branches, depending on how you like the branches looking. I skipped around some to get my branches lined up where I wanted them. You can't mess up this pattern, so don't worry about not skipping the same amount of posts between branches!

Do 2 spiraling rows like this,

and then we make the branches even smaller.

Next 2 rounds will go like this;

dc, ch1

dc, ch1

dc, ch2

dc, ch1

dc, ch1

Now you can do a row or two of;

dc, ch1

dc, ch1

dc, ch1

dc, ch1

and while getting near the top now, you will want to start doing hdc's.

hdc, ch1

hdc, ch2

hdc, ch1

and skip only 1-2 posts between branches now.

Finished Tree

This inside of the tree you can stuff with poly-fill if you like, or just crochet a circle bottom for it, or it's fine as is even.

Here's my finished tree.....

and that silly boy again :):):)

Ornaments, Lights and Stars!

I bought these last year for the first tree I made. They were from Joann's but any craft store will have them.

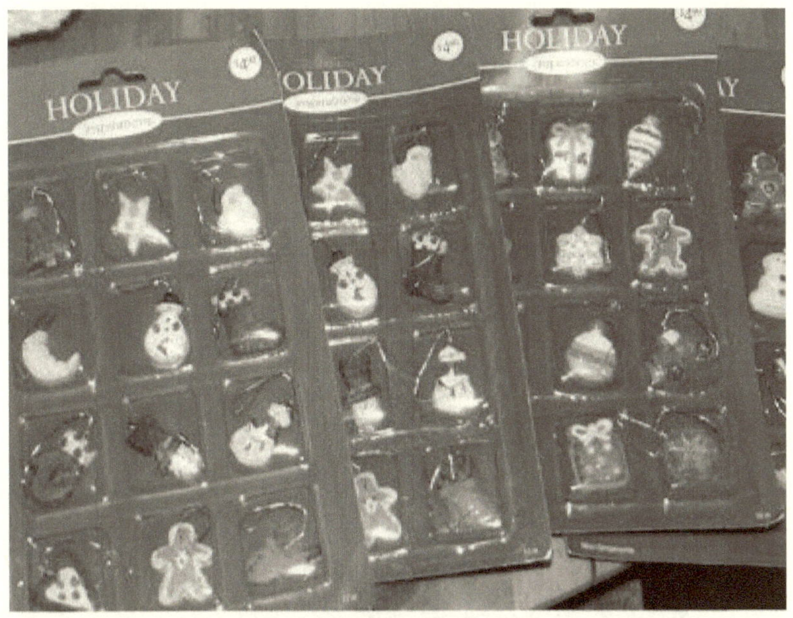

The stars you can put the stick part right thru the tiny hole on top the tree!

Those little presents are so cute!

I used a rainbow variegated yarn to make a garland looking somewhat like lights. Looks good on the darker tree.

This one I made last year. The branches are a little smooshed from being stored.

That silly little boy again! :)

Here is the light green one from last year, the dark green one I just made, and the white one which is 2 strands, so it's a little bigger.

Christmas Trees

Material: Fingering cotton yarn

Hook: 2,5 mm

Measure: 8x10h cm aprox.

Abbreviations:

ch: chain

sc: single crochet

hdc: half double crochet

dc: double crochet

2-dc-tog: 2 double crochet stichs closed together

3-chs-picot: 3 chains closed picot

5-chs-picot: 5 chains closed picot

sl.st: slip stitch

st/s: stitch/ es

rnd: round

rep **: repeat from * to *

Begin with an adjustable ring.

Round 1: Ch 2 and make 1 dc in the ring (count as first 2-dc-tog). *Ch 3 and make 1 2-dc-tog in the ring*; rep ** a total of 8 times. Ch 1 and make 1 hdc on the top of the first st in this rnd. Adjust the ring. (Total: 9 2-dc-tog in this rnd).

Round 2: Ch 1 and make 1 sc. Ch 4, skip next st and make 1 sc in the next 3 chs. Ch 2, make 1 5-chs-picot and ch 2, skip next st and make 1 sc in the next 3 chs. *Ch 4, skip next st and make 1 sc in the next 3 chs; ch 4, skip next st and make 1 sc in the next 3 chs. Ch 2, make 1 5-chs-picot and ch 2, skip next st and make 1 sc in the next 3 chs.* Rep ** one more time. Ch 2 and make 1 hdc on the top of the first st in this rnd.

Round 3: Ch 1 and make 1 sc. Ch 4, skip next st and make 1 sc in the next 4 chs; ch 4, skip next st and make 1 sc in the 5-chs-picot; ch 4 and make 1 sc in the 5-chs-picot. *Ch 4, skip next st and make 1 sc in the next 4 chs; ch 4, skip next st and make 1 sc in the next 4 chs. Ch 4, skip next st and make 1 sc in the next 5-chs-picot*. Rep ** one more time. Ch 4 and join to the first st of the rnd with 1 sl.st.

Round 4: Ch 3 (counted as first dc in this rnd) and make 1 3-chs-picot. Make 4 dc in the next 4 chs; make 1 dc + 1 3-chs-picot in the next st; make 4 dc in the next 4 chs; make 1 dc + 1 3-chs-picot in the next st. In the next 4 chs: Make 3 dc, ch 25, make 1 sl.st in the last dc, and make 2 dc. Make 1 dc + 1 3-chs-picot in the next st. *Make 4 dc in the next 4 chs; make 1 dc + 1 3-chs-picot in the next st*; rep ** a total of 3 times. In the next 4 chs, make: 2 dc, 1 dc + 1 3-chs-picot, 2 dc. Make 1 dc in the next st. *Make 4 dc in the next 4 chs; make 1 dc in the next st*; rep ** total of 3 times. In the next 4 chs, make: 2 dc, 1 dc + 1 3-chs-picot, 2 dc. Make 1 dc + 1 3-chs-picot in the next st. Make 4 dc in the next 4 chs. Join to the first st of the rnd with 1 sl.st. Fasten off.

To make the Tree Trunk:

Insert the hook in the dc st shown in red color in the chart to take a loop.

Row 1: Ch 1 and make 1 sc in the same st. Make 1 sc in each of the next 5 sts. Turn the work.

Row 2: Ch and make 1 sc in the first. Make 1 sc in each st of the row. Turn the work.

Row 3: Ch 1 and make 3 sc in the first st. Make 1 sc in each of the next 4 sts. Make 2 sc in the last st of the row. Fasten off.

CROCHET CHRISTMAS TREE GARLAND

This free Christmas tree garland crochet pattern, uses the following US crochet stitches and terms:

(ch) Chain, (sc) Single Crochet, (hdc) Half Double Crochet, (spl-hdc) Split Half Double Crochet – explained below.

Numbers shown in ( ) indicates the number of stitches you should have at the end of the row/round.

To help you read this pattern, the commas represent each stitch or the number of stitches after x. A number shown before a stitch, means work that number of stitches in the same next stitch making an increase. For example; {dc x3, 2dc,} would mean work a dc into next 3 stitches, and 2 dc sts in the same following stitch.

SPLIT HDC STITCH:

For this pattern, we will be using a Split Half Double Crochet stitch. This stitch creates an even, leafy effect, texture while making the piece thicker and sturdier.

To work a Split Half Double Crochet (spl-hdc), you work a normal hdc stitch into the middle of the legs of the previous row, instead if the usual stitch tops.

The legs of the stitch are the V shape created under the stitch tops. You will yarn over as usual, then insert your hook in through the middle of the V shape, coming out through the centre of the V shape on the other side as well, yarn over and pull up a loop, yarn over and pull through all 3 loops on hook.

I have highlighted the V shapes on the image below:

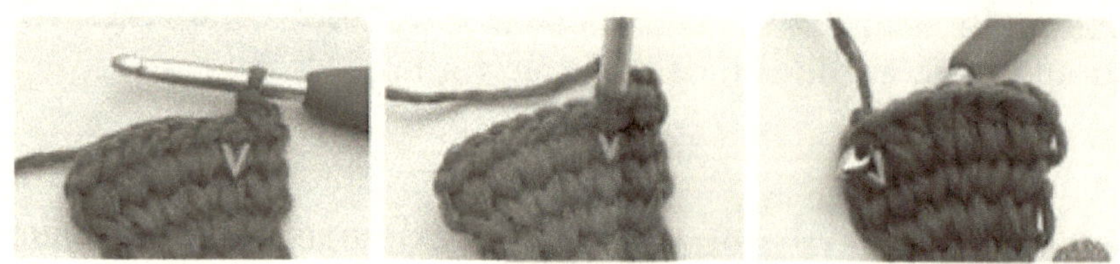

It may be tricky to find the right place for your stitches when starting off, the first 2 stitches can be hard to see. Just insert your hook and check the back to see if it looks right.

You will be working under 3 loops, the normal top 2 loops (front and back loops) and the back bar loop of the hdc stitch.

You'll find it easier to locate the right place as you work more rows.

Christmas Tree Ornament

Beginning ch1s are turning chains only and will not count as stitches.

Using Green yarn, start by chaining 2, ,

R1.

2hdc into the first ch going under the top loop and back bump of the chain to avoid over-stretching, turn (2)

R2.

ch1, 2spl-hdc in each st, turn (4)

R3.

ch1, spl-hdc in each st, turn (4)

R4.

ch1, spl-hdc, 2spl-hdc x2, spl-hdc, turn (6)

R5.

ch1, spl-hdc in each st, turn (6)

R6.

ch1, spl-hdc x2, 2spl-hdc x2, spl-hdc x2, turn (8)

R7.

ch1, spl-hdc in each st, turn (8)

R8.

ch1, spl-hdc x3, 2spl-hdc x2, spl-hdc x3, turn (10)

R9.

ch1, spl-hdc in each st, turn (10)

R10.

ch1, spl-hdc x4, 2spl-hdc x2, spl-hdc x4, turn (12)

R11.

ch1, spl-hdc in each st (12)
Fasten off Green yarn.

Now add the trunk.

We will use the back loop and back bar of the spl-hdc stitches, leaving the front loop to form a neat separation line.

With the front of the last row still facing you, join Brown yarn with a sl st through the back loop and back bar of the 5th st along,

R1.

Continue in the back loops and back bars only, ch1, hdc in the same st as join, hdc x3, turn (4)

R2.

ch1, spl-hdc x4, turn (4)

R3.

For this finishing row, work into the same split stitch location, but work single crochets instead. ch1, sc x4 (4)

Fasten off and weave in all ends.

CONGRATULATIONS!

You have completed your mini Christmas Tree ornament, you can now decorate it if desired. Make as many as you like and string them together to make a festive decorative garland, use them individually as hanging decorations, or use them as a finishing touch on gift wrapping.

GARLAND JOIN:

I have joined my trees with a crocheted chain. You could use ribbon or string instead. I have joined 9 trees, creating a garland just over 1 meter long. You can adjust the number of trees or spacing between trees to suit your own decor.

Start by chaining 30, sc into the top of a tree, *ch 15, sc into the top of the next tree,* repeat between * for each tree, and finish by chaining 30.

AMIGURUMI CHRISTMAS TREE

Christmas tree is a lovely decoration at Christmas time. Embellished with spangles, beads, buttons or pearls it makes an eye-catching home decoration for yourself or as a gift.

Quick and easy project, made in one piece.

Height: about 12 cm

Supplies:

– worsted (10 ply) or DK (8 ply) weight yarn – some green and a little bit of brown. I used different mixtures of cotton, linen, bamboo and wool. All of them look nice, but give a slighly different feeling.

– crochet hook 3.5 mm

– polyester fiberfill

– flower pot base (Ø 5.5 cm)

– some spangles, beads, pearls or buttons for embellishing

Abbreviations

sc – single crochet, st(s) – stitch(es), rep – repeat

WORK IN CONTINUOUS ROUNDS. DO NOT JOIN OR TURN UNLESS OTHERWISE INSTRUCTED.

IT WOULD BE WISE TO USE A STITCH MARKER AND PLACE IT IN THE FIRST STITCH OF EACH ROUND TO MARK THE BEGINNING OF IT.

PATTERN

Crocheted in one piece from top to down.

1: Green. Start with 6 sc in a magic ring.

2: Sc in each st around

3: (sc in next st, 2 sc in next st) rep 3 times = 9

4: Sc in each st around

5: (sc in each of next 2 sts, 2 sc in next st) rep 3 times = 12

6: Sc in each st around

7: (sc in each of next 3 sts, 2 sc in next st) rep 3 times = 15

8: Sc in each st around

9: (sc in each of next 4 sts, 2 sc in next st) rep 3 times = 18

10: Sc in each st around

11: (sc in each of next 5 sts, 2 sc in next st) rep 3 times = 21

12: Sc in each st around

13: (sc in each of next 6 sts, 2 sc in next st) rep 3 times = 24

14: Sc in each st around

15: (sc in each of next 3 sts, 2 sc in next st) rep 6 times = 30

16: Sc in each st around

17: (sc in each of next 4 sts, 2 sc in next st) rep 6 times = 36

18: Sc in each st around

19: Working in the back loops only, sc in each st around

20: (sc in each of next 2 sts, sc2tog) rep 9 times = 27

21: (sc in next st, sc2tog) rep 9 times = 18

Start filling with fiberfill and add stuffing as the work progresses.

22: (sc in next st, sc2tog) rep 6 times = 12

23-27: Brown. Working in the back loops only, sc in each st around

28: 2 sc in each st = 24

29: Sc in each st around

Embellish the tree and glue it onto the pot base.

www.ingramcontent.com/pod-product-compliance
Lightning Source LLC
Chambersburg PA
CBHW030410160726

47992CB00007B/3046